THE LITTLE
BOOK OF
SCOTTISH
JOKES

THE LITTLE BOOK OF SCOTTISH JOKES

Copyright © Summersdale Publishers Ltd, 2017

With research by Agatha Russell, Giada Nizzoli and Norman Ferguson

Illustrations © tskoy, Panda Vector, RedKoala, Billy Read / Shutterstock

Summersdale Publishers Ltd
46 West Street
Chichester
West Sussex
PO19 1RP
UK

www.summersdale.com

Printed and bound in Malta

ISBN: 978-1-78685-213-7

Substantial discounts on bulk quantities of Summersdale books are available to corporations, professional associations and other organisations. For details contact general enquiries: telephone: +44 (0) 1243 771107 or email: enquiries@summersdale.com.

THE LITTLE BOOK OF SCOTTISH JOKES

Greig Findlay

summersdale

A GLASWEGIAN GOES
INTO A BAKERY.
HE POINTS AT THE
CABINET AND ASKS,
'IS THAT A DOUGHNUT
OR A MERINGUE?'

THE BAKER REPLIES,
'NO, YOU'RE RIGHT,
IT'S A DOUGHNUT.'

As the Earth is being formed God is designing Scotland. An angel watches him creating the wonderful coasts, the magnificent mountains and the cool running waters of its rivers. The angel says to God, 'Are you not making it a bit too perfect?' To which God replies, 'Wait till you see who their neighbours are!'

A Scotsman, in planning his new house, left the roof off one room. A friend asked the reason for this.

'Oh,' said the Scotsman, 'that's the shower.'

There are ten cows in a field. Which one of them is on holiday?

The wan wae the wee calf.

An American tourist was lost in the Scottish Highlands. He meandered around for a whole week until he bumped into a local man wearing a kilt. 'Thank the Lord I have met you, I've been lost for a week out here.'

'Is there a reward for your rescue?' enquired the local.

'I don't think so.'

'I'm afraid that you are still lost then,' came the reply.

A woman and a man from Aberdeen were stranded on a desert island after a shipwreck. Their clothes were in rags and their food was running out.

'I suppose it could always be worse,' said the woman.

'Oh, aye, it could,' agreed the Aberdonian. 'I might have bought a return ticket.'

A regiment of Roman soldiers are advancing north of Hadrian's Wall. They see a Pictish warrior up ahead who's taunting them. The Roman commander sends a platoon out after him. From over the hill come the sounds of fierce battling. A lone centurion eventually appears, weary and bloodied. 'Sire, we must send more troops!'

So another squad is sent: similar battling noises are heard before another centurion appears, again all bruised and battered. 'Sire, we need more men!'

Off another squad goes until half an hour later, after more fighting being heard, a centurion crawls back. The commander says to him, 'What is going on? Why can't my brave men defeat a single enemy?'

'Sire. We were wrong. There're two of them!'

After the England vs Scotland match there were 12,000 beer cans left in London by the Scottish fans.

All three culprits were arrested.

A MAN WALKS INTO A BUTCHER'S SHOP ON A COLD DAY TO THE WELCOME SIGHT OF AN ELECTRIC HEATER WITH BOTH BARS ON BEHIND THE COUNTER.

WHILE EYEING UP THE MEATS, HE ASKS, 'IS THAT YOUR AYRSHIRE BACON?'

'NO,' REPLIES THE BUTCHER, 'IT'S ONLY MY HANDS I'M WARMING.'

A thoughtful Scotsman, Tavish, was going out to the pub. He turned to his wife and asked her to get her coat and scarf on.

'Tavish, you lovely man, are you taking me to the pub with you?'

'Nah,' he replied. 'While I'm out, I'm going to turn the heating off.'

Ewan takes a pair of shoes back to the shop and complains that there is a lace missing.

'No,' argues the assistant, 'look at that – it says Taiwan.'

Jock put up posters around the town that read:

Missing: £5 note. Of sentimental value.

For Duncan's birthday gift Finlay got him a fine hunting hat with earflaps. Duncan was delighted and always fastened the earflaps down with the straps underneath his chin. One day Finlay noticed that Duncan wasn't wearing his hat and he asked why.

'I've stopped wearing the hat ever since the accident,' Duncan explained.

'What accident?'

'Well, a man offered me a swig of whisky and I had the earflaps down so I didn't hear a word of what he said.'

Kenny discovered that hearing aids were rather expensive, so he came up with an ingenious idea. He cut off his telephone flex and wrapped it over his ear. He couldn't hear any better, but people tended to shout when they spoke to him.

Mungo walked into a pub and said in a shaky voice, 'Is anyone in here the owner of that Doberman outside?'

'I am the owner,' announced a large biker.

'Oh dear! I think my Scottish terrier just killed him.'

'That's not possible. How could a little runt of a Scotty kill my Doberman?'

Mungo mumbled, 'Well, the thing is, it appears that he got stuck down your dog's throat.'

Have you heard the tale of the Grand Canyon?

Legend says it was created by a Scotsman on holiday who lost his coin in a ditch.

Rory and Angus were taking a trip to London. While sightseeing they saw a sign in a shop window that read: 'Suits £5.00 Shirts £3.00 Socks 50p.'

'Angus! Wait there, I've spotted some bargains – we could make a fortune back in Scotland.' Rory enters the shop and says in his best British accent, 'Hello there my good sir, I would like to order ten suits, fifteen shirts and twenty socks.'

'Are you Scottish?' said the man behind the counter.

'Yes, how did you guess?'

'Because this is a dry cleaner.'

Patricia's son said that he had made it into the school play. 'What part?' she asked.

'I play the part of the Scottish husband.'

'No, you go back to your teacher and tell her that you at least want a speaking part!'

A psychology teacher began the class by asking her students a question. 'Everyone who thinks they are stupid, please would you stand up?' A few moments passed and Hamish stood up. The teacher said, 'Hamish, do you think you're stupid?'

He replied, 'No Miss, but I don't want to leave you standing there all by yourself.'

Fergus stops before a tombstone in his local cemetery and reads what it says.

HERE LIES A LAWYER AND
A TRUTHFUL MAN.

'Achh, no,' says Fergus, 'Surely there's not enough room for two men in that wee grave?'

'HOW'S YOUR NEW FLAT IN LONDON?' ASKED ROSS'S MOTHER DURING THEIR WEEKLY PHONE CALL.

'IT'S ALRIGHT, BUT THERE'S A LADY NEXT DOOR WHO KEEPS WAILING AND THEN THE MAN THE OTHER SIDE KEEPS BANGING HIS HEAD REALLY HARD AGAINST THE WALL.'

'DON'T TAKE ANY NOTICE OF THEM, ROSSY. DON'T LET THEM GET YOU DOWN – JUST IGNORE THEM.'

'AYE, MUM I DO. I JUST KEEP PLAYING MA BAGPIPES.'

How many Scotsmen does it take to change a light bulb?

Och! It's no that dark!

The Queen is on a tour of a Scottish hospital. She is shown into a ward with a number of people with no obvious signs of injury or disease. She greets the first patient and the chap replies: 'Fair fa' your honest sonsie face, great chieftain o' the puddin'-race!'

The Queen is bemused. She goes to the next patient and greets him. The patient replies: 'Some hae meat, and canna eat, and some wad eat that want it, but we hae meat and can eat, and sae the Lord be thankit.'

The third starts rattling off as follows: 'Wee sleekit, cow'rin, tim'rous beastie, O, what a panic's in thy breastie!'

The Queen turns to the doctor and asks, 'What sort of ward is this? A mental ward?'

'No,' replies the doctor, 'it's the Burns Unit.'

A Scotsman was reported to the police for making irritating phone calls.

He kept reversing the charges.

An officer in the Scots Guards, pinned down with his men in Italy in 1944, urgently signalled his commanding officer:

'Need reinforcements to rescue us. Send six tanks or one piper.'

**Duncan: Drinking
makes you look more
beautiful, Morag.**

**Morag: But I haven't
had a drink.**

Duncan: No, but I have.

IF YOU WERE LOST OUT IN
THE WILDERNESS, WHO
WOULD YOU TRUST FOR
DIRECTIONS: AN IN-TUNE
BAGPIPE PLAYER, AN OUT-
OF-TUNE BAGPIPE PLAYER
OR FATHER CHRISTMAS?

THE OUT-OF-TUNE BAGPIPE
PLAYER. THE OTHER
TWO INDICATE YOU'VE
BEEN HALLUCINATING.

My mother used to tell me, 'Before you assess a man, walk to Glasgow in his shoes.'

'And why's that?'

'Well after that who cares? He's miles away and you've got his shoes.'

Hamish decided to
call his father-in-law
'the Exorcist' because
every time he came
to visit he made the
spirits disappear.

Gordon walks into a pub with an Englishman and an Irishman. The barman looks up and says, 'What the hell is this? Some sort of joke?'

There is a little-known fact on the origin of copper wire: it was invented by two Aberdonians fighting over a penny.

On the Isle of Skye one beautiful evening, after ten years of dating Sandy, Jean thought at last it was time to ask the question herself.

'Sandy,' she breathed, 'is it not about time we were getting married?'

After a heavy silence, Sandy sighed. 'Aye, Jean, it is. But who would have us?'

A woman goes into the local newspaper to place a death notice for her husband. She writes down what she wants: 'Jim Smith, from Peterhead. Dead.' and hands over her money. The newspaper clerk says to her, 'For that amount you can put more words down.' She takes back the bit of paper, thinks for a moment, writes, then hands it back. It now reads, 'Jim Smith, from Peterhead. Dead. Ford Escort for sale.'

What's the difference between the Loch Ness Monster and an easy-going Englishman?

Maybe one day we'll find Nessie.

Why did the chocolate bar melt?

Because it was Bounty.

What's the difference between a Scotsman and a canoe?

A canoe sometimes tips.

How do you keep a Scotsman interested after marriage?

Wear perfume that smells of whisky.

Why don't the employees of the Scottish Parliament look out of the window in the morning?

They'd have nothing to do in the afternoon.

'Well, Mr Allaway, your last daughter has been married off. Are you pleased?'

'I feel wonderful! The confetti was starting to disintegrate.'

Gordon won the
EuroMillions and yet he had
a very long face. When he
was asked why he looked
this way he replied, 'Aye,
it really upsets me to think
of the money I wasted
on the second ticket.'

A young man announced that he was getting married. He explained that he would be wearing a kilt and his friend asked, 'And what's the tartan?'

He replied, 'Oh, she'll be wearing a white dress obviously.'

A Scot walks into an antiques fair and asks a dealer, 'How much for the antlers?'

He says, 'Two hundred and fifty quid for those.'

'That's affa dear.'

The vendor replies, 'Aye, yer right about that.'

A tourist in Edinburgh sees a kilted bagpiper and goes up to him. 'Excuse me, I have to ask, is anything worn under the kilt?'

'No, ma'am,' he replies. 'It's all in perfect working order.'

What do you call a Scottish parrot?

A MacCaw

Did you hear about what the English, Irish and Scottish did when they heard that the world would end?

The English went out and got sozzled, the Irish went to church and the Scottish had a closing-down sale.

A small boy fell into the River Clyde but was saved from drowning by a passer-by. When the hero dried out a little, the boy's father came over to him.

'Are you the man that saved my laddie?'

'Aye.'

'Where's his bonnet then?'

**THERE ONCE WAS
A SCOTSMAN WHO
WAS SO DESPERATELY
IN NEED OF SOME
MONEY THAT HE
HAD TO WITHDRAW
SOME FROM HIS OWN
BANK ACCOUNT.**

An Englishman provoked by a Scot's ridicule of his nationality said, 'I was born an Englishman and I shall die and Englishman.'

The Scot replied, 'Man, ain't yer got no ambition?'

How do you get a highlander on top of the roof?

Tell him the drinks are on the house.

A man went to a private Scottish doctor and said, 'Doc, I've got a poor memory. What do you advise?'

'Well,' said the Doc, 'for a start you can pay me in advance.'

A SCOTTISH FARMER WAS
HARVESTING HIS CROP
OF POTATOES WHEN
AN AMERICAN TOURIST
WALKED RIGHT UP TO HIM
AND SAID, 'IN ALABAMA
WE GROW POTATOES
SIX TIMES LARGER.'

THE SCOTSMAN CALMLY
REPLIED, 'AH, BUT WE
JUST GROW THEM TO THE
SIZE OF OUR MOUTHS.'

How many bagpipe players does it take to change a light bulb?

Five. One to manage the bulb and the other four to tell him how much better they could have done it.

A Scotsman, an Englishman and an Australian were in a bar and had just started on a new round of drinks when a fly landed in each glass of beer.

The Englishman took his out on the blade of his Swiss Army knife.

The Australian blew his away in a cloud of froth.

The Scotsman lifted his one up carefully by the wings and held it above his glass. 'Go on,' he growled, 'Spit it oot, ye wee devil!'

'Sandy suggested a candlelit dinner last night,' Jessie reported to her friend the next day.

'That was dead romantic,' she said.

'Not really,' sighed Jessie. 'It just saved him having to fix the fuse.'

Mungo returned to the office after a fishing trip. He was telling the office staff about the size of one of the fish that he had caught.

'I'll bet it was almost as big as the Loch Ness monster,' jeered his boss.

'Loch Ness monster?' replied the fisherman. 'Man, I was using the monster for bait!'

Angus took a girl back home in a taxi. She was so pretty that he could hardly take his eyes off the meter.

Billy McNab was once run over by a brewery truck.

It was the first time for years that the drink had been on him.

How can you tell the difference between Bing Crosby and Walt Disney?

Bing sings, but Walt disnae.

A Londoner goes to an Aberdeen bar and is surprised to find the beer only two pence a pint. The barman explains that it's the price to mark the centenary of the pub opening. The visitor notices, however, that the bar is empty.

'Are the regular customers not enjoying the special prices?' he asks.

To which the barman replies, 'Naw, they're waiting for happy hour.'

THE OLD SCOTTISH WOMAN
LAY DYING. SHE LOOKED UP
AND ASKED HER HUSBAND IF HE
WOULD DO HER JUST ONE SMALL
FAVOUR BEFORE SHE PASSED ON.

'FINLAY?' SHE ASKED. 'ON THE
DAY OF THE FUNERAL I WOULD
LIKE YOU TO RIDE IN THE SAME
COACH AS MY MOTHER.'

TO WHICH HER HUSBAND
REPLIED, 'ALL RIGHT, FLO. I WILL
DO THAT JUST TO PLEASE YOU.
BUT YOU HAVE COMPLETELY
SPOILT THE DAY FOR ME.'

An Englishman, an Irishman and a Scotsman were each left £5,000 from a now deceased but rich friend, on the condition that they each put £100 into his coffin, just in case he needed it in the afterlife.

Both the Englishman and the Irishman put their money into the coffin. The Scotsman took the cash out again and replaced it with a £300 cheque.

Donald: Have you ever seen one of those machines that can tell when a person is lying?

Sandy: Aye, I married one!

Why do pipers march when they play?

To get as far away from the noise as possible.

Callum stood at the altar, swaying from side to side.

'This man is drunk!' complained Father MacDonald.

'I know, Father,' said the bride. 'But sure he wouldn't have come if he was sober!'

Two Scotsmen met 25 years after their last get-together. They hugged and slapped each other's back and tears formed in their eyes as they renewed their old friendship.

'Let's have a drink like we did in the old days,' the first Scot winked at his mate.

'Aye,' his mate replied. 'And don't forget it's your shout.'

**Fergus moved to London
and annoyed his English
acquaintances by boasting about
how great Scotland was.**

**Finally, an irate Englishman asked,
'If Scotland is so marvellous,
why didn't you stay there?'**

'Well,' explained Fergus, 'they
are all so clever up there that I
had to come down here to have
any chance of making it at all.'

'Crivvens!' said Donald. 'I was teaching the wife to drive and the brakes failed when we came down the hill.'

'What did you do?'

'I told her to try to hit something cheap!'

Jimmy decided to get married, so one morning he sent messages to three girls, proposing marriage. Two phoned immediately to say 'Yes', while the third phoned that night to say the same.

He married the third girl saying, 'The lass for me is the one who waits for the cheap rates.'

Did you know that the first people in the UK to have double-glazing were the Scots?

It was so their bairns couldn't hear the ice-cream vans.

A ROBBER STICKS HIS GUN
IN A SCOTSMAN'S RIBS AND
DEMANDS, 'YOUR MONEY
OR YOUR LIFE!' WHEN
AFTER A MOMENT THERE IS
NO ANSWER, HE REPEATS
HIS DEMAND: 'YOUR
MONEY OR YOUR LIFE!'

'HOLD ON!' THE
SCOTSMAN REPLIES. 'I'M
THINKING IT OVER!'

McDougal walks into a fish and chip shop. 'I want ten pence worth of chips, please. I want lots of salt and vinegar on them and two pence worth of pickled onions. And wrap the whole lot in today's newspaper.'

Fiona and Gregor were playing
golf with Cameron and Isla at
St Andrews when a club official
had to come and break up a fight.

'What's the problem here?' he said.

'Well,' said Fiona, 'Gregor's had
a stroke and Cameron wants
to add it to my score.'

The Scots have an infallible cure
for sea-sickness: they lean over
the side of the ship with a ten
pence coin in their teeth.

Old Sandy McPherson was dying. Tenderly, his wife Maggie knelt by his bedside and asked, 'Have ye no' a last wish, Sandy?'

Faintly came the answer: 'A wee bit of yon boiled ham.'

'Wheesht, man,' said Maggie, 'ye ken fine that's for the funeral.'

'If William "Braveheart" Wallace was alive today he would be looked on as a remarkable man.'

'Aye, of course he would! He'd be more than seven hundred years old!'

Hamish was taking his girlfriend for a drive on his motorbike.

As they passed a hot-dog stand she sighed, 'My, those hot dogs smell really nice.'

'Hold on a moment,' said Hamish with great gallantry. 'I'll drive a little closer so you can get a better whiff.'

At an art auction in Edinburgh, a wealthy Englishman lost his wallet containing £10,000 in cash. He announced to the gathering that he would give a reward of £100 to the person who found it.

From the back of the hall a Scottish voice declared, 'I'll give ye £150.'

An American oilman was sent to the Isle of Lewis on a month's contract. He arrived on a grey, cloudy, rainy day. He woke up the next morning to find it was grey, cloudy and raining. The next day it was the same, and the next.

One day, as he came out of his room to find it was grey, cloudy and raining, he saw a small boy passing and cried in exasperation, 'Does the weather ever change here?'

'I really don't know,' said the child. 'I'm only ten years old.'

What did the conjoined twins from Glasgow call their autobiography?

Oor Wullie.

Wife: Don't you think, dear, that a man has more sense after he is married?

Husband: Yes dear, but it's too late then.

A man returned to his native town in Scotland after having been in the US for twenty years. He was greeted at the airport by his brother, who had a beard down to his knees.

The returning Scot asked, 'What are you doing with the long beard?'

The bearded brother grumbled, 'When you left, you took the razor with you!'

A Scottish lad and lass were sitting together on a hill in the Highlands. They had been silent for a while when the lass said, 'A penny for yer thoughts, Lachlan.'

The lad was a bit abashed, but he finally said, 'Well, Alison, I was thinkin' how nice it would be if ye'd give me a wee bit of a kiss.'

So she did. But again he lapsed into a pensive mood which lasted long enough for the lass to ask him, 'What are ye thinkin' now, Lachlan?'

'Well, I was hopin' ye hadn't forgotten that penny!'

**DONALD: DO YOU SERVE
BREAKFAST HERE?**

**WAITRESS: YES, WHAT
WOULD YOU LIKE?**

**DONALD: LUMPY PORRIDGE
AND SOME BURNT TOAST.**

**WAITRESS: WHATEVER
YOU SAY, SIR.**

**DONALD: NOW, ARE YOU
DOING ANYTHING WHILE
THAT'S BEING MADE?**

WAITRESS: WHY – NO, SIR.

**DONALD: THEN SIT HERE AND NAG
ME AWHILE. I'M HOMESICK.**

A man was walking through Glasgow's Blythswood Square when he was approached by a woman of the night. She asked him if he'd like some 'super sex'.

He thought for a moment then replied: 'I don't know... What kind of soup is it?'

**If an Englishman
is seen taking off
wallpaper in his house,
he is redecorating.**

**If a Scotsman is seen
taking off wallpaper,
he is relocating.**

After discovering they had won £15 million on the lottery, Mr and Mrs McFlannel sat down to discuss their future.

Mrs McFlannel announced, 'After twenty years of washing other people's stairs, I can throw my old scrubbing brush away at last.'

Her husband agreed. 'Of course you can, hen. We can easily afford to buy you a new one now.'

There was a collision
between two taxis
in Edinburgh.

All 27 passengers
were injured.

Did you hear about the
Scotsman who told his
son that the gas meter
was a savings bank and
he should put his pocket
money in it every week?

One day Finlay bought a bottle of fine whisky and while walking home he fell over. While getting up he felt something wet on his trousers.

He looked up to the sky and shouted, 'Oh Lord, please, I beg you: let it be blood!'

A Scotsman phones a dentist to enquire about the cost of a tooth extraction.

'Eighty-five pounds, sir.'

'Eighty-five! Whit aboot if ye didnae use any anaesthetic?'

'That'd be painful, but I could knock fifteen pounds off.'

'Whit aboot if ye used one of your dentist trainees, no anaesthetic and make it a trainin' session, with the other students watchin'?'

'That'd be good for the students. I guess I'd only charge you ten pounds, but I must warn you: it'll be traumatic!'

'Och, now yer talkin' laddie!' said the Scotsman. 'Can ye confirm an appointment for the wife next Tuesday?'

Leonard went down to the airport to pick up his friend Hamish. When he got there, he found him terribly upset.

'I lost the best part of my baggage on the way here.'

'Did you misplace it on the plane or was it stolen?' asked Leonard.

'No,' said Hamish, 'the cork came out.'

A cute Highland girl was giving
a manicure to a man in a barber
shop in Dunkeld. The man asked,
'How about a date later?'

'I'm married,' she said.

'So call up your husband and tell him
you're going to visit a girlfriend.'

She replied, 'You tell him yourself:
he's shaving your throat.'

A Scottish woman goes to the dentist for a check-up. The dentist asks her to take a seat and asks 'Comfy?'

'Govan,' she replies.

Teacher: Can anyone use the word 'fascinate' in a sentence?

Jimmy: My dad bought a new shirt with nine buttons, but he's so fat he can only fasten eight.

'McDOUGALL'S DEAD.
HE FELL INTO A VAT
OF WHISKY.'

'OH NO, WHAT A SHAME.
WAS IT A QUICK DEATH?'

'I DON'T THINK SO. HE
CAME OUT TWICE TO
GO TO THE CLUDGIE!'

Jock was out working the field when an aeroplane landed nearby.

'I'll give you a ride for five pounds,' said the pilot.

'Sorry, cannae afford it,' replied Jock.

'Tell you what,' said the pilot, 'I'll give you and your wife a free ride if you promise not to yell. Otherwise it'll be ten pounds.'

So up they went and the pilot rolled, looped, stalled and did all he could to scare Jock. Nothing worked and the defeated pilot finally landed the plane.

Turning around to the rear seat he said, 'I have to hand it to you. For country folk you are brave!'

'Aye,' said Jock, 'but ye nearly had me there when the wife fell oot!'

A Scot was describing a frightful moment to his old friend.

'There was I in the water. I was going down for the second time. The water kept pulling me down, and I went under for the third time. Just then, my whole life flashed in front of me. It was one picture after another.'

His friend asked, 'Did any of them happen to show you borrowing a fiver from me ten years ago?'

McTavish was traveling by rail in America. He asked the railway clerk for a ticket to Springfield.

'Which Springfield, sir?' asked the clerk. 'Missouri, Ohio, or Massachusetts?'

'Which is nearest?'

'Sir, my wife said I was
to ask for a pay rise,'
said Alexander.

'Good,' said his boss.
'I'll ask my wife if I
should give you one.'

**An Aberdonian was ill
with scarlet fever.**

'Send for my creditors,'
he said. 'I can give them
something at last.'

Gavin is digging peat at his croft when a passing American tourist asks, 'How much land do you have here?'

'About two acres,' Gavin replies.

'You know, back home it takes me a day to drive around my ranch!' the American boasts.

'Aye,' says Gavin. 'I once had a car like that.'

CALUM WROTE A COMPLAINT TO THE EDITOR OF HIS LOCAL NEWSPAPER. IT READ: 'DEAR SIR, IF YOU PRINT ANY MORE JOKES ABOUT SCOTSMEN I WILL STOP BORROWING YOUR NEWSPAPER!'

A Scotsman driving home one night ran into a car driven by an Englishman. The Scotsman got out of the car to apologise and offered the Englishman a drink from a bottle of whisky. The Englishman was glad to have a drink.

'Go on,' said the Scot, 'have another drink.'

The Englishman drank gratefully. 'But don't you want one, too?'

'Aye,' replied the Scotsman, 'but only after the police have gone.'

A Kirkcaldy undertaker sent a telegram to a bereaved man, telling him his mother-in-law had died and asking whether he wanted her embalmed, cremated or buried.

Back came the reply: 'All three – tak' nae chances.'

A bus company in Fife decided to offer a cheaper concessionary fare to frequent travellers so that, for a pound, they got six journeys instead of four. An old gentleman was outraged, though.

'It's all dam' foolishness,' he declared. 'Now I've got to walk to town six times instead of four to save a pound!'